My Keto Recipes

Tasty, Easy to Follow, and Healthy Ketogenic recipes to lose weight Safely and Healthy. Start now to Burn the excess fat. The Ketogenic cookbook for absolute beginners made simple.

Susy Baggins

Table of Contents

1. Coconut Panna Cotta with Raspberries

2. Ricotta Parfait with Strawberries

3. Minty Coconut Parfait with Cranberries

4. Healthy Chia Pudding With Strawberries

5. Chocolate Candies with Blueberries

Basic and Easy to Follow Keto Recipes

Super Guacamole

Servings 2

Ingredients

- ½ tbsp fresh cilantro, chopped

- 1 avocado, peeled, pitted

- ¼ yellow onion, minced

- ¼ lime, juiced

- ½ tomato, peeled, chopped

- Salt and chili powder to taste

Prep + Cooking Time: 10 min

How to start:

1. Mash the avocado with a fork in a bowl.

2. Mix in the onion, lime juice, tomato, chili powder, and salt.

3. Sprinkle with cilantro and serve

Nutritional value (per serving):

Cal 172;

Carbs 1.3g;

Fat 15.5g;

Protein 2.2g

Cheese and Bacon Bomb

Servings: 4 fat bombs

Ingredients for 2

- ¼ cup Chèvre cheese, grated

- 2 tbsp butter, softened

- ¼ cup cream cheese, softened

- 4 bacon slices, chopped

Prep + Cooking Time: 44 min

How to start:

1. Fry the bacon in a skillet over medium heat for 4,30 min.

2. Grease a baking sheet with the bacon fat and set aside.

3. In a bowl, stir together the Chèvre cheese, cream cheese, butter, and stir-fried bacon until well blended.

4. Roll the mixture into 4 "balls" and place them on the sheet.

5. Freeze for 30 minutes.

Nutritional value (per serving)

Cal 281

Net Carbs 0.2 g

Fat 25 g

Protein 10 g

Avocado Boats with Eggs and Bacon

Servings: 2

Ingredients

- ½ tsp smoked paprika

- 1 avocado, halved and pitted

- 2 eggs

- 1 bacon slices, chopped

- 1 tbsp chives, chopped

- Salt and black pepper to taste

Prep + Cooking Time: 25/26 min

How to start:

1. Preheat the oven to 360 F.

2. Scoop out some of the avocado flesh into a bowl.

3. Place the avocado halves in a greased baking dish and crack an egg into each half.

4. Season with paprika, salt, and black pepper and sprinkle with bacon.

5. Bake for 15-16 minutes or until set.

6. Top with fresh chives

7. Serve.

Nutritional value (per serving):

Cal 318

Fat 27 g

Carbs 0.7 g

Protein 12 g

Simply Avocado Fries with Chipotle Mayo Sauce

Servings: 2

Ingredients:

- ¼ cup mayonnaise

- ¼ cup olive oil

- 1 avocados, sliced

- 1 cup almond flour

- 1 tbsp lemon juice

- 2 large eggs, beaten

- 2 chipotle sauce

- Salt and black pepper to taste

Prep + Cooking Time: 21 min

1. Mix the almond flour with salt and black pepper.

2. Toss avocado slices in the eggs and then dredge in the flour mixture.

3. Heat olive oil in a deep pan and fry the avocado slices until golden brown, 2-3 minutes per side.

4. In a bowl, mix the mayonnaise, chipotle sauce, lemon juice, and salt.

5. Serve the fries with the sauce.

Nutritional value (per serving):

Cal 632

Carbs 2.8 g

Fat 59 g

Protein 10 g

Pigs in Blankets

Servings: 2

Ingredients

- 4 thin bacon slices

- 4 Vienna sausages

Prep + Cooking Time: 29/30 min

How to start:

1. Preheat oven to 360 F.

2. Wrap each sausage tightly with a slice of bacon.

3. Lay the bacon-wrapped sausages on a greased baking sheet and roast for 18-20 minutes until the bacon is crisp and golden.

4. Top with rosemary.

Nutritional value (per serving):

Cal 621

Net Carbs 0.1 g

Fat 57 g

Protein 30 g

Avocado Mousse and Bacon

Servings: 2

Ingredients:

- ¼ lime, juiced and zested

- ½ cup sour cream

- 1 ripe avocado, pitted, halved

- 2 oz bacon, sliced

- 1 tbsp cilantro, chopped

- Salt and black pepper to taste

Prep + Cooking Time: 14/15 min

How to start:

1. Set a skillet over medium heat and stir-fry the bacon until crispy, about 5/6 minutes.

2. Transfer to a paper towel to soak up the excess fat.

3. In a bowl, mix the avocado flesh, sour cream, lime juice, lime zest, salt, and pepper.

4. Stir until everything is well mixed and smooth.

5. Spoon the mousse into glass cups and top with bacon and fresh cilantro.

6. Serve warm

Nutritional value (per serving):

Cal 480

Carbs 0.5 g

Fat 42 g

Protein 13 g

Smoked Salmon and Scrambled Eggs

Servings: 2

Ingredients:

- 1 tbsp butter

- 4 eggs

- 1 tbsp fresh dill, chopped

- 2 oz smoked salmon, chopped

- ¼ cup sour cream

- Salt and black pepper to taste

Prep + Cooking Time: 14/15 min

How to Start:

1. Whisk the eggs into a medium bowl along with sour cream, salt, and pepper.

2. Melt the butter in a skillet over medium heat and add the eggs, stirring quickly.

3. Lower the heat and gently mix them with a spatula;

4. Cook until the eggs are barely set, 2-3 minutes.

5. Remove from heat and stir in the salmon.

6. Top with dill and serve.

Nutritional value (per serving):

Cal 274

Carbs 0.6 g

Fat 21 g

Protein 18 g

Egg Muffins with Bacon and Cheddar

Servings: 2

Ingredients:

- 1 oz cheddar cheese, grated

- 1 tbsp sour cream

- 2 bacon slices

- ½ green onion, chopped

- 2 eggs

- ½ tsp red chili flakes

Prep + Cooking Time: 15/16 min

How to start:

1. Place the bacon on a preheated skillet over medium heat and cook for 2 minutes per side; set aside.

2. Grease 4 ovenproof cups with the bacon fat.

3. Line the bottom and the sides of the cups with the bacon slices.

4. Spread half of the cheese over, and cover with sour cream.

5. Carefully crack an egg into each cup and finish with the remaining cheese.

6. Place the cups in the microwave for 1-2 minutes until the cheese melts.

7. Sprinkle with green onion and red chili flakes

8. Serve.

Nutritional value (per serving):

Cal 120

Carbs 0.4 g

Fat 9 g

Protein 9 g

Avocado "Carbonara"

Servings: 2

Ingredients:

- ½ teaspoon onion powder

- Juice of 1/3 lemon

- ¼ teaspoon garlic powder

- ¼ cup olive oil

- ½ avocado, peeled and pitted

- 1 eggs, beaten

- 1 cups cream cheese

- 2 ½ tbsp psyllium husk

- 1 cup coconut cream

- Salt and black pepper to taste

- ¼ cup grated Parmesan

- 2 tbsp toasted pecans

Prep + Cooking Time: 29 min

How to Start:

1. Preheat oven to 300 F.

2. In a bowl, add the eggs, cream cheese, psyllium husk, and salt to taste.

3. Whisk until smooth batter forms.

4. Line a baking sheet with wax paper, pour in the batter, and cover with another wax paper.

5. Use a rolling pin to flatten the dough into the sheet.

6. Bake for 12 minutes, then take off the wax papers and slice the "pasta" into thin strips lengthwise.

7. Cut each piece into halves, pour into a bowl, and set aside.

8. In a blender, combine avocado, coconut cream, lemon juice, onion and garlic powders and puree until smooth.

9. Pour olive oil over the "pasta" and stir to coat.

10. Pour the avocado sauce on top and mix well.

11. Sprinkle with salt, pepper, and freshly grated Parmesan cheese.

12. Garnish with toasted pecans and serve.

Nutritional value (per serving):

Cal 768

Carbs 9 g

Fat 55 g

Protein 34 g

Golden Saffron Cauli Rice

Servings: 2

Ingredients:

- 1 tbsp chopped parsley

- 1 cups cauli rice

- ½ tbsp butter

- A pinch of saffron soaked in ¼-cup almond milk

- 1 tbsp olive oil

- 3 garlic cloves, sliced

- ½ yellow onion, thinly sliced

- ¼ cup vegetable broth

- Salt and black pepper to taste

Prep + Cooking Time: 14/15 min

How to start:

1. Warm olive oil in a saucepan over medium heat and fry garlic until golden brown but not burned; set aside.

2. Sauté butter and onion in the saucepan for 3 minutes.

3. Stir in cauli rice.

4. Remove the saffron from the milk and pour the milk and stock into the saucepan.

5.   Mix, cover, and cook for 5 minutes.

6.   Season with salt, black pepper, and parsley.

7.   Fluff the cauli rice and dish into serving plates.

8.   Garnish with the fried garlic and serve.

Nutritional value (per serving):

Cal 88

Carbs 5.8 g

Fat 7 g

Protein 3 g

Pasta Puttanesca and zucchini

Servings: 2

Ingredients**:**

- 1/2 tbsp capers, chopped

- 1 garlic clove, sliced

- ¼ tsp dried oregano

- 2 anchovies in olive oil, drained

- 1 lb zucchinis, spiralized

- 1 tbsp olive oil

- 1 tbsp fresh basil, chopped

- ¼ tsp cayenne pepper

- ¼ cup black pitted olives, halved

- 1 (7-oz) cans diced tomatoes

- ¼ cup Parmesan cheese, grated

- Salt and black pepper to taste

Prep + Cooking Time: 28 min

How to Start:

1. Warm the olive oil in a saucepan and toss in zucchini; stir
   quickly for about 1 minute.

2. Season to taste and set aside.

3. To the saucepan, add garlic, cayenne pepper, oregano, capers, and anchovies; cook for 2-4 minutes until the anchovies melt into the oil.

4. Pour in tomatoes and simmer for 10-12 minutes, stirring often, until the sauce thickens slightly; season.

5. Pour the sauce over zucchini pasta and top with olives, Parmesan cheese, and basil to serve.

Nutritional value (per serving):

Cal 185

Carbs 6.8 g

Fat 10 g

Protein 12 g

Five Seed Crackers

Servings: 5 (30 crackers)

Ingredients:

- ¼ cup almond flour

- ¼ cup sesame seeds

- ¼ cup chia seeds

- 2 tbsp coconut oil, melted

- 1 tsp flax seeds

- ¼ cup pumpkin seeds

- ¼ cup sunflower seeds

- 1 tsp psyllium husk powder

- 1 tsp salt

- ¾ cup boiling water

Prep + Cooking Time: 29/30 min

How to start:

1. Preheat oven to 350 F.

2. Combine almond flour with the seeds, psyllium husk, and salt. Pour in coconut oil and boiling water and mix until a dough forms with a gel-like consistency.

3. Line a baking sheet

4. with parchment paper and place the dough on the sheet.

5. Cover with another parchment paper and with a rolling pin to flatten into the baking sheet.

6. Remove the parchment paper from the top.

7. Use a pizza cutter to cut the dough into 1-inch squares.

8. Bake for 15-20 minutes, or until golden.

9. Serve cooled.

Nutritional value (per serving):

Cal 71

Carbs 3 g

Fat 5.5 g

Protein 2.7 g

Ketogenic Mac and Cheese

Servings: 2

Ingredients:

- ½ tsp garlic paste

- ½ cup cream cheese

- 1 tbsp butter, melted

- 2 zucchinis, spiralized

- Salt and black pepper, to taste

- ½ cup heavy cream

Prep + Cooking Time: 20/21 min

How to Start:

1. Top the zucchinis with melted butter, salt, and pepper and toss to coat.

2. Cook in a saucepan over medium heat for 5-6 minutes.

3. Remove to a serving plate.

4. In the same pan, pour the heavy cream, garlic paste, and cream cheese and heat through, stirring frequently.

5. Reduce heat to low and simmer for 2-3 minutes or until the sauce thickens.

6. Adjust the seasoning.

7. Coat the zucchinis in the cheese sauce serve

Nutritional value (per serving):

Cal 687

Fat 71 g

Carbs 3.8 g

Protein 11 g

Asparagus and Mediterranean Salmon

Servings: 2

Ingredients:

- ½ lemon, sliced thinly

- 2 salmon fillets

- ½ tsp dried dill

- 2 tbsp olive oil

- ½ tsp garlic powder

- ½ lemon, juiced

- ½ lb asparagus, trimmed

- Salt and black pepper to taste

Prep + Cooking Time: 31 min

How to start:

1. Preheat the oven to 390 F.

2. In a bowl, mix 1 tbsp of olive oil, dill,

3. garlic powder, salt, and pepper.

4. Rub the mixture onto the salmon.

5. Place the fish on a lined baking sheet.

6. Drizzle with lemon juice.

7. Brush the asparagus with the remaining olive oil and season with salt and pepper.

8. Arrange asparagus around the salmon.

9. Roast for 13-15 minutes, until the salmon fillets flake easily with a fork.

10. Serve topped with lemon slices.

Nutritional value (per serving):

Cal 382

Fat 24 g

Carbs 2.4 g

Protein 35 g

Speedy Salmon with Creamy Parsley Sauce

Servings: 2

Ingredients:

- 1 tbsp mayonnaise

- 1 tbsp parsley, chopped

- 2 salmon fillets

- 1 cup heavy cream

- ½ lemon, zested and juiced

- 1 tbsp Parmesan cheese, grated

- Salt and black pepper to taste

Prep + Cooking Time: 24 min

How to start:

1. In a bowl, mix the heavy cream, parsley, mayonnaise, lemon zest, lemon juice, salt, and pepper; set aside.

2. Season the fish with salt and black pepper, drizzle lemon juice on both sides of the fish, and arrange the fillets on a parchment paper-lined baking sheet.

3. Spread the mayo-parsley mixture and sprinkle with Parmesan cheese.

4. Bake in the oven for 15 minutes at 380 F.

5. Great served with steamed broccoli.

Nutritional value (per serving):

Cal 555

Fat 29 g

Carbs 2.1 g

Protein 57 g

Breakfast Recipes

Crespelle with Mascarpone

Servings 2

Ingredients:

- ½ cup almond milk
- 1 tsp baking powder
- 1 tsp vanilla extract
- 2 tsp liquid stevia
- 1 large egg
- ¼ cup olive oil
- ½ cup almond flour
- 1 tsp mint, chopped
- Whole raspberries to garnish
- 1 cup mascarpone cheese

Prep + Cooking Time: 34 min

How to start:

1. Beat the egg in a bowl.

2. Add in the almond milk, vanilla extract, and half of the stevia and stir to combine.

3. In another bowl, whisk the almond flour and baking powder together.

4. Then, pour the egg mixture into the almond flour mixture and continue whisking until smooth.

5. Heat olive oil in a pan over medium heat and pour in 1 soup spoon of batter.

6. Cook on one side for 2 minutes, flip the pancake, and cook the other side for 2 minutes.

7. Transfer the pancake to a plate and repeat the cooking process until the batter is exhausted.

8. Mix the mascarpone with the remaining stevia and mint in a small bowl.

9. Spread each mini pancake with mascarpone and scatter raspberry over to serve.

Nutritional value (per serving):

Cal 688

Fat 60 g

Carbs 5.1 g

Protein 22 g

Pancakes with Buttermilk

Servings 2

Ingredients

- ½ vanilla pod

- ½ lemon, juiced

- ¼ cup buttermilk

- 2 eggs

- ¼ cup almond flour

- ¼ tsp baking powder

- ½ tbsp Swerve

- 1 tbsp unsalted butter

- 1 tbsp olive oil

- 2 tbsp sugar-free maple syrup

- Greek yogurt

- Blueberries

Prep + Cooking Time: 24/25 min

How to start:

1. In a small bowl, whisk the buttermilk, lemon juice, and eggs.

2. In another bowl, mix almond flour, baking powder, and Swerve.

3. Fold in the egg mixture and whisk until smooth.

4. Cut the vanilla pod open and scrape the beans into the flour mixture. Stir to incorporate evenly.

5. In a skillet, melt a quarter of the butter and olive oil and spoon in 2 tablespoons of the pancake mixture into the pan.

6. Cook for 4 minutes or until small bubbles appear.

7. Flip and cook for 2 minutes or until set and golden.

8. Repeat the cooking until the batter finishes using the remaining butter and olive oil in the same proportions.

9. Plate the pancakes, drizzle with maple syrup, top with a generous dollop of yogurt, and scatter some blueberries on top.

Nutritional value (per serving):

Cal 173

Carbs 1.5 g

Fat 11 g

Protein 7,5 g

Tasty Ginger Pancakes

Servings 2

Ingredients:

- 1 egg
- 2 tbsp Swerve
- ¼ tsp baking soda
- 1 cup almond flour
- 1 tsp cinnamon powder
- 1 tsp ginger powder
- 1 cup almond milk
- 2 tbsp olive oil
- Lime sauce
- ¼ cup liquid stevia
- ½ lime, juiced and zested
- 2 tbsp butter
- ½ tsp arrowroot starch

Prep + Cooking Time: 20/21 min

How to start:

1. Combine together the almond flour, cinnamon powder, Swerve,
2. baking soda, ginger powder, egg, almond milk, and olive oil in a mixing bowl.
3. Heat oil in a skillet over medium heat and spoon 2-3 tablespoons of the mixture into the skillet.
4. Cook the batter for 1 minute, flip it and cook the other side for another minute.

5. Remove the pancake onto a plate and repeat the cooking process until the batter is exhausted.

6. Mix the stevia and arrowroot starch in a saucepan.

7. Set the pan over medium heat and gradually stir 1 cup water until it thickens, about 1 minute.

8. Turn the heat off and add the butter, lime juice, and lime zest. Stir the mixture until the butter melts.

9. Drizzle the sauce over the pancakes and serve warm.

Nutritional value (per serving):

Cal 342

Fat 24 g

Carbs 6 g

Protein 8.5 g

Belgium Waffles and Cheese

Servings: 2

Ingredients

- 3 eggs
- ½ cup almond milk
- 2 tbsp liquid stevia
- 2 tbsp olive oil
- ½ cup almond flour
- ½ cup cream cheese, softened
- 1 lemon, zested and juiced

Prep + Cooking Time: 24 min

How to Start:

1. In a bowl, combine the cream cheese, lemon juice, lemon zest, and stevia.
2. In a separate bowl, whisk the olive oil, almond milk, and eggs.
3. Stir in almond flour and combine until no lumps exist. Let the batter sit for 5 minutes to thicken.
4. Spritz a waffle iron with a cooking spray.
5. Ladle a ¼ cup of the batter into the waffle iron and cook for about 5 minutes.
6. Repeat with the remaining batter. Slice the waffles into
7. quarters;
8. Apply the lemon spread in between each of two waffles, snap
9. Serve.

Nutritional value (per serving):

Cal 321

Fat 25 g

Carbs 7.6 g

Protein 11 g

Pancakes with Spinach and Feta Cheese

Servings 2

Ingredients:

- 2 tbsp coconut milk
- ½ tsp baking powder
- ½ cup almond flour
- ½ cup feta cheese, crumbled
- ½ cup spinach, chopped
- 1 egg, beaten

Prep + Cooking Time: 21 min

How to Start:

1. In a medium bowl, put the egg, almond flour, baking powder, feta, coconut milk, and spinach and whisk to combine.
2. Set a skillet over medium heat for a minute.
3. Fetch a soup spoonful of the mixture and cook for 2 minutes.
4. Flip the pancake and cook further for 1 minute.
5. Remove onto a plate and repeat the cooking process until the batter is exhausted.
6. Serve with your favorite topping.

Nutritional value (per serving):

Cal 411

Fat 31 g

Carbs 6 g

Protein 11 g

Waffles with Jalapeno, Avocado and Bacon

Servings 4

Ingredients:

- 3 tbsp butter, melted
- ½ cup almond milk
- 1 ½ tbsp almond flour
- Salt and black pepper to taste
- 1 tsp parsley, chopped
- 1 jalapeño pepper, minced
- 6 eggs
- 1 cup cheddar, crumbled
- 6 slices bacon, chopped
- 2 avocados, sliced

Prep + Cooking Time: 21 min

How to Start:

1. In a skillet over medium heat, fry the bacon until crispy, about 5 minutes.
2. Remove to a plate. In a bowl, combine the remaining ingredients, except for the avocado.
3. Preheat waffle iron and grease with cooking spray.
4. Pour in the batter and close the lid.
5. Cook for 5 minutes or until the desired consistency is reached.
6. Do the same with the rest of the batter. Top with avocado and bacon.

Nutritional value (per serving):

Cal 770

Fat 68 g

Carbs 7 g

Protein 28 g

Pastrami Gofres and Peanut Butter

Servings 3

Ingredients:

- 5 tbsp coconut flour

- 5 oz pastrami, chopped

- 1 tsp dried rosemary

- 5 eggs

- 1 tsp baking soda

- 3 tbsp peanut butter, melted

- ½ tsp salt

- 4 tbsp tomato puree

Prep + Cooking Time: 21 min

How to start:

1. Preheat your waffle iron to high.

2. In a mixing bowl, thoroughly whisk the eggs, rosemary, and salt.

3. Stir in the coconut flour, baking soda, and peanut butter.

4. Continue whisking until everything is well incorporated.

5. Add a third of the batter to the waffle iron and cook for 3 minutes until golden.

6. Repeat with the remaining batter.

7. Spread the tomato puree over each gofre and top with pastrami. Serve.

Nutritional value (per serving):

Cal 410

Fat 26 g

Carbs 4.1 g

Protein 26 g

Savory Waffles with Tomato and Cheese

Servings 4

Ingredients:

- 1 cup Gouda cheese, grated
- 2 tomato, sliced
- 4 eggs, beaten
- 4 tbsp sour cream
- ½ tsp allspice
- Salt and black pepper, to taste

Prep + Cooking Time: 19/20 min

How to start:

1. Mix the eggs, allspice, black pepper, salt, and sour cream in a shallow bowl.
2. Add in the shredded cheese.
3. Spritz a waffle iron with a cooking spray. Pour in half of the batter. Cook for 5 minutes until golden.
4. Repeat with the remaining batter.
5. Serve with tomato slices.

Nutritional value (per serving):

Cal 255

Fat 19 g

Carbs 1.6 g

Protein 18 g

Nuts with Zesty Zucchini Bread

Servings 2

Ingredients:

- 2 eggs
- 1/3 cup coconut flour
- 1 tsp baking powder
- 1/2 cup butter, softened
- 1/2 cup erythritol
- 1/3 cup ground almonds
- ½ lemon, zested and juiced
- ½ cup finely grated zucchini
- ½ cup whipped cream
- ½ tbsp chopped hazelnuts

Prep + Cooking Time: 50 min + cooling time

How to start:

1. Preheat oven to 380 F.
2. Grease a springform pan with and line with parchment paper.
3. Set aside. In a bowl, beat the butter and erythritol until creamy and pale.
4. Add eggs one after another while whisking.
5. Add in coconut flour and baking powder and stir along with ground almonds, lemon zest, juice, and zucchini.
6. Spoon the mixture into the pan.
7. Bake for 40 minutes or until risen and a toothpick inserted into the cake comes out clean.
8. Let cool inside the pan for 10 minutes.
9. Transfer to a wire rack.

10. Spread whipped cream on top and sprinkle with hazelnuts.

11. Serve and enjoy!.

Nutritional value (per serving):

Cal 780

Carbs 3.6 g

Fat 70

Protein 33 g

Cheese, Bacon and Avocado Mug Cakes

Servings 4/5

Ingredients:

- 1/2 cup almond flour
- 4 eggs
- 1 cup flax meal
- 4 tbsp buttermilk
- 4 tbsp pesto
- Salt and black pepper, to taste
- 3 tbsp ricotta cheese
- 3 oz bacon, sliced
- 2 avocados, sliced

Prep + Cooking Time: 15 minutes

How to start:

1. Whisk eggs, buttermilk, and pesto in a bowl.
2. Season with salt and pepper.
3. Gently add in flax meal and almond flour and divide the
4. mixture between two greased ramekins. Place in the microwave and cook for 1-2 minutes.
5. Leave to cool slightly before filling.
6. In a nonstick skillet over medium heat, cook the bacon until crispy, about 5 minutes; set aside.
7. Invert the ramekins onto a plate and cut in half, crosswise.
8. Assemble the sandwiches by spreading ricotta cheese and topping with bacon and avocado slices.

Nutritional value (per serving):

Cal 489;

Fat 38 g

Carbs 4 g

Protein 18 g

Bread with Zucchini and Pumpkin

Servings 2

Ingredients:

- 1/2 cup pumpkin, shredded
- ½ cup zucchini, shredded
- 1/4 cup coconut flour
- 3 eggs
- 1/2 tbsp olive oil
- ¾ tsp baking soda
- ½ tbsp cinnamon powder
- ¼ tsp salt
- ¼ cup buttermilk
- ½ tsp apple cider vinegar

Prep + Cooking Time: 58 min

How to Start:

1. Preheat oven to 360 F.
2. In a bowl, mix all the ingredients and stir to form a dough.
3. Pour the batter into a greased loaf pan and bake for 45 minutes or until a toothpick comes out clean.
4. Let cool for 5 minutes.
5. Serve sliced.

Nutritional value (per serving):

Cal 201

Fat 11 g

Carbs 4.4 g

Protein 11 g

Keto Sandwiches with Ham and Cheese

Servings 4

Ingredients:

- 5 eggs
- 1 tsp baking powder
- 1 tbsp psyllium husk powder
- 3 slices mozzarella cheese
- 3 slices smoked ham
- 6 tbsp butter, softened
- 4 tbsp almond flour

Prep + Cooking Time: 21 min

How to start:

1. To make the buns, whisk together almond flour, baking powder, 4
2. tbsp of butter, husk powder, and eggs in a bowl; mix until a dough
3. forms.
4. Place the batter in two oven-proof mugs and microwave for 2
5. minutes or until firm.
6. Remove, flip the buns over, cool, and cut in
7. half.
8. Put a slice of mozzarella cheese and a slice of ham on one bun half
9. and top with the other.
10. Warm the remaining butter in a skillet.
11. Add sandwiches and grill until the cheese is melted.
12. Enjoy!

Nutritional value (per serving):

Cal 515

Fat 4

Carbs 2.2 g

Protein 22 g

Raspberries and Almond Cakes

Servings 2

Ingredients:

- 1 cup almond flour
- 1 tsp baking soda
- 1/2 tsp vanilla extract
- 1 ½ tbsp almond flakes
- ¼ tsp salt
- 1 tbsp liquid stevia
- 6 oz cream cheese, softened
- ¼ cup butter, melted
- 1 egg
- 8 raspberries
- 1/2 cup almond milk

Prep + Cooking Time: 36 minutes

How to Start:

1. Mash the raspberries with a fork and set aside.
2. Mix the almond flour, baking soda, vanilla, and salt in a large bowl. In a separate bowl, whisk the egg and almond milk.
3. Add in the cream cheese, stevia, and butter and beat until well incorporated.
4. Fold in the flour and mashed raspberries and spoon the batter into greased muffin cups two-thirds way up.
5. Top with almond flakes.
6. Bake for 20 minutes at 400 F until golden brown, remove to a wire rack to cool slightly for 5 minutes before serving.

Nutritional value (per serving):

Cal 353

Fat 32 g

Carbs 8.7 g

Protein 9.3 g

Salads & Soups

Pasta with Roasted Red Pepper Sauce

Preparation time: 10 minutes

Cooking time: 12 minutes

Servings: 4

Ingredients

- ¾ cup soy milk

- 1 tablespoon olive oil

- ¾ teaspoon salt

- 1 (12 oz) jar roasted red pepper

- 4 garlic cloves, chopped

- 2 tablespoons tahini

- 2 tablespoons nutritional yeast

- ½ teaspoon red pepper flakes

- 12 oz penne pasta

Directions:

1. Fill a suitably-sized pot with salted water and bring it to a boil on

high heat.

2. Add pasta to the boiling water and cook until it is al-dente, then

rinse under cold water.

3. Add drained roasted red peppers, garlic, salt, olive oil, soy milk,

tahini, nutritional yeast, and red pepper flakes to a blender then

puree until smooth.

4. Add the pepper puree to a pan along with salt and black

pepper.

5. Cook the puree for 5 minutes on a simmer.

6. Add cooked pasta to the sauce and mix well.

7. Serve warm.

Pasta with White Beans and Olives

Preparation time: 20 minutes

Cooking time: 10 minutes

Servings: 2

Ingredients:

- Basil, fresh, ground, one quarter cup

- Black olives, two tablespoons chop

- Black pepper, one half teaspoon

- Cannellini beans, one fifteen ounce can, drain and rinse

- Garlic, minced, one tablespoon

- Olive oil, one tablespoon

- Romano cheese, fresh, grated, two tablespoons

- Tomatoes, two medium-sized diced

- Ziti or rigatoni, whole wheat, four ounces

Directions:

1. Follow the instructions on the packaging to cook the quinoa. Cook the beans and garlic in hot oil for five minutes. Remove the pan from the heat. Add to the beans and garlic the basil, olives, pepper, and tomatoes and mix well. Place the cooked pasta on two plates divided evenly and tops the pasta with the tomato and bean mix, then sprinkle on the cheese and serve.

Plant Based Keto Lo Mein

Preparation Time: 10 minutes

Cooking Time: 10 minutes

Servings: 2

Ingredients:

- 2 tablespoons carrots, shredded
- 1 package kelp noodles, soaked in water
- 1 cup broccoli, frozen
- For the Sauce
- 1 tablespoon sesame oil
- 2 tablespoons tamari
- ½ teaspoon ground ginger
- ¼ teaspoon Sriracha
- ½ teaspoon garlic powder

Directions:

1. Put the broccoli in a saucepan on medium low heat and add the sauce ingredients.

2. Cook for about 5 minutes and add the noodles after draining water.

3. Allow to simmer about 10 minutes, occasionally stirring to avoid burning.

4. When the noodles have softened, mix everything well and dish out to serve.

Vegetarian Chowmein

Preparation Time: 20 minutes

Cooking Time: 30 minutes

Servings: 2

Ingredients:

- ½ large onion, chopped
- ½ small leek, chopped
- ½ tablespoon ginger paste
- ½ tablespoon Worcester sauce
- ½ tablespoon Oriental seasoning
- ½ teaspoon parsley
- Salt and black pepper, to taste
- ½ pound noodles
- 2 large carrots, diced
- 2 celery sticks, chopped
- 1 tablespoon olive oil
- ½ teaspoon garlic paste
- 1½ tablespoons soy sauce
- 1 tablespoon Chinese five spice
- ½ teaspoon coriander
- 2 cups water

Directions:

1. Put olive oil, ginger, garlic paste, and onion in a pot on medium heat and sauté for about 5 minutes.

2. Stir in all the vegetables and cook for about5 minutes.

3. Add rest of the ingredients and combine well.

4. Secure the lid and cook on medium heat for about 20 minutes, stirring occasionally.

5. Open the lid and dish out to serve hot.

Veggie Noodles

Preparation Time: 10 minutes

Cooking Time: 5 minutes

Servings: 2

Ingredients:

- 2 tablespoons vegetable oil

- 4 spring onions, divided

- 1 cup snap pea

- 2 tablespoons brown sugar

- 9 oz. dried rice noodles, cooked

- 5 garlic cloves, minced

- 2 carrots, cut into small sticks

- 3 tablespoons soy sauce

Directions:

1. Heat vegetable oil in a skillet over medium heat and add garlic and 3 spring onions.

2. Cook for about 3 minutes and add the carrots, peas, brown sugar and soy sauce.

3. Add rice noodles and cook for about 2 minutes.

4. Season with salt and black pepper and top with remaining spring onion to serve.

Stir Fry Noodles

Preparation Time: 10 minutes

Cooking Time: 8 minutes

Servings: 4

Ingredients:

- 1 cup broccoli, chopped
- 1 cup red bell pepper, chopped
- 1 cup mushrooms, chopped
- 1 large onion, chopped
- 1 batch Stir Fry Sauce, prepared
- Salt and black pepper, to taste
- 2 cups spaghetti, cooked
- 4 garlic cloves, minced
- 2 tablespoons sesame oil

Directions:

1. Heat sesame oil in a pan over medium heat and add garlic, onions, bell pepper, broccoli, mushrooms.

2. Sauté for about 5 minutes and add spaghetti noodles and stir fry sauce.

3. Mix well and cook for 3 more minutes.

4. Dish out in plates and serve to enjoy.

Spicy Sweet Chili Veggie Noodles

Preparation Time: 10 minutes

Cooking Time:7 minutes

Servings: 2

Ingredients:

- 1 head of broccoli, cut into bite sized florets
- 1 onion, finely sliced
- 1 tablespoon olive oil
- 1 courgette, halved
- 2 nests of whole-wheat noodles
- 150g mushrooms, sliced
- For Sauce
- 3 tablespoons soy sauce
- ¼ cup sweet chili sauce
- 1 teaspoon Sriracha
- 1 tablespoon peanut butter
- 2 tablespoons boiled water

For Topping

- 2 teaspoons sesame seeds
- 2 teaspoons dried chili flakes

Directions:

1. Heat olive oil on medium heat in a saucepan and add onions.

2. Sauté for about 2 minutes and add broccoli, courgette and mushrooms.

3. Cook for about 5 minutes, stirring occasionally.

4. Whisk sweet chili sauce, soy sauce, Sriracha, water and peanut butter in a bowl.

5. Cook the noodles according to packet instructions and add to the vegetables.

6. Stir in the sauce and top with dried chili flakes and sesame seeds to serve.

Creamy Vegan Mushroom Pasta

Preparation Time: 10 minutes

Cooking Time: 30 minutes

Servings: 6

Ingredients:

- 2 cups frozen peas, thawed
- 3 tablespoons flour, unbleached
- 3 cups almond breeze, unsweetened
- 1 tablespoon nutritional yeast
- ⅓ cup fresh parsley, chopped, plus extra for garnish
- ¼ cup olive oil
- 1 pound pasta of choice
- 4 cloves garlic, minced
- ⅔ cup shallots, chopped
- 8 cups mixed mushrooms, sliced
- Salt and black pepper, to taste

Directions:

1. Take a bowl and boil pasta in salted water.

2. Heat olive oil in a pan over medium heat.

3. Add mushrooms, garlic, shallots and ½ tsp salt and cook for 15 minutes.

4. Sprinkle flour on the vegetables and stir for a minute while cooking.

5. Add almond beverage, stir constantly.

6. Let it simmer for 5 minutes and add pepper to it.

7. Cook for 3 more minutes and remove from heat.

8. Stir in nutritional yeast.

9. Add peas, salt, and pepper.

10. Cook for another minute and add

11. Add pasta to this sauce.

12. Garnish and serve!

Vegan Chinese Noodles

Preparation Time: 15 minutes

Cooking Time: 8 minutes

Servings: 4

Ingredients:

- 300 g mixed oriental mushrooms, such as oyster, shiitake and
- enoki, cleaned and sliced
- 200 g thin rice noodles, cooked according to packet instructions
- and drained
- 2 garlic cloves, minced
- 1 fresh red chili
- 200 g courgettes, sliced
- 6 spring onions, reserving the green part
- 1 teaspoon corn flour
- 1 tablespoon agave syrup
- 1 teaspoon sesame oil
- 100 g baby spinach, chopped
- Hot chili sauce, to serve
- 2(1-inch) pieces of ginger
- ½ bunch fresh coriander, chopped
- 4 tablespoons vegetable oil
- 2 tablespoons low-salt soy sauce
- ½ tablespoon rice wine
- 2 limes, to serve

Directions:

1. Heat sesame oil over high heat in a large wok and add the mushrooms.

2. Sauté for about 4 minutes and add garlic, chili, ginger, courgette, coriander stalks and the white part of the spring onions.

3. Sauté for about 3 minutes until softened and lightly golden.

4. Meanwhile, combine the corn flour and 2 tablespoons of water in a bowl.

5. Add soy sauce, agave syrup, sesame oil and rice wine to the corn flour mixture.

6. Put this mixture in the pan to the veggie mixture and cook for about 3 minutes until thickened.

7. Add the spinach and noodles and mix well.

8. Stir in the coriander leaves and top with lime wedges, hot chili sauce and reserved spring onions to serve.

Vegetable Penne Pasta

Preparation Time: 15 minutes

Cooking Time: 20 minutes

Servings: 6

Ingredients:

- ½ large onion, chopped
- 2 celery sticks, chopped
- ½ tablespoon ginger paste
- ½ cup green bell pepper
- 1½ tablespoons soy sauce
- ½ teaspoon parsley
- Salt and black pepper, to taste
- ½ pound penne pasta, cooked
- 2 large carrots, diced
- ½ small leek, chopped
- 1 tablespoon olive oil
- ½ teaspoon garlic paste
- ½ tablespoon Worcester sauce
- ½ teaspoon coriander
- 1 cup water

Directions:

1. Heat olive oil in a wok on medium heat and add onions, garlic and ginger paste.

2. Sauté for about 3 minutes and stir in all bell pepper, celery sticks, carrots and leek.

3. Sauté for about 5 minutes and add remaining ingredients except for pasta.

4. Cover the lid and cook for about 12 minutes.

5. Stir in the cooked pasta and dish out to serve warm.

Spaghetti in Spicy Tomato Sauce

Preparation Time: 15 minutes

Cooking Time: 40 minutes

Servings: 4

Ingredients:

- 1 pound dried spaghetti
- 1 red bell pepper, diced
- 4 garlic cloves, minced
- 1 teaspoon red pepper flakes, crushed
- 2 (14-ounce) cans diced tomatoes
- 1 (6-ounce) can tomato paste
- 2 teaspoons vegan sugar, granulated
- 2 tablespoons olive oil
- 1 medium onion, diced
- 1 cup dry red wine
- 1 teaspoon dried thyme
- ½ teaspoon fennel seed, crushed
- 1½ cups coconut milk, full-fat
- Salt and black pepper, to taste

Directions:

1. Boil water in a large pot and add pasta.

2. Cook according to the package directions and drain the pasta into a colander.

3. Dish out the pasta in a large serving bowl and add a dash of olive oil to prevent sticking.

4. Heat 2 tablespoons of olive oil over medium heat in a large pot and add garlic, onion and bell pepper.

5. Sauté for about 5 minutes and stir in the wine, thyme, fennel and red pepper flakes.

6. Allow to simmer on high heat for about 5 minutes until the liquid

is reduced by about half.

7. Add diced tomatoes and tomato paste and allow to simmer for about 20 minutes, stirring occasionally.

8. Stir in the coconut milk and sugar and simmer for about 10 more minutes.

9. Season with salt and black pepper and pour the sauce over the pasta.

10. Toss to coat well and dish out in plates to serve

Poultry and Pork Recipes

Chicken Dippers with Homemade Ketchup

Servings 4

Ingredients

- 1 lb chicken breasts, cut into strips
- 14 oz canned tomatoes, diced
- 1 tbsp tomato paste
- ½ tbsp xylitol
- 1 tbsp balsamic vinegar
- 1 cup tomato sauce
- 1 tbsp basil, chopped
- ½ cup almond flour
- ¼ cup Parmesan, grated
- ½ tsp garlic powder
- 1 tsp dried parsley
- ½ tsp dried thyme
- Salt and black pepper to taste
- 1 egg, beaten in a bowl
- 2 tbsp olive oil

Directions + Total Time: 34 min

1. Place a saucepan over medium heat.

2. Add the tomatoes, tomato paste, xylitol, tomato sauce, salt, pepper, and balsamic vinegar and bring to a boil.

3. Cook for 10-15 minutes, stirring frequently until thickened.

4. Adjust the seasoning.

5. Top the ketchup with basil and set aside.

6. In a bowl, combine the almond flour, parsley, Parmesan, pepper, garlic powder, thyme, and salt.

7. Dip the chicken strips in the egg and then in the almond flour mixture.

8. Heat a pan over medium heat and warm the olive oil.

9. Fry the chicken until golden, about 4-6 minutes.

10. Remove to paper towels to soak the excess oil.

11. Serve with ketchup.

Cal 336;

Fat 21g;

Carbs 7.7g;

Protein 25g

Winter Chicken with Vegetables

Servings 2

Ingredients

- 2 tbsp olive oil

- 2 cups whipping cream

- 1 lb chicken breasts, chopped

- 1 onion, chopped

- 1 carrot, chopped

- 2 cups chicken stock

- Salt and black pepper, to taste

- 1 bay leaf

- 1 turnip, chopped

- 1 parsnip, chopped

- 1 cup green beans, chopped

- 2 tsp fresh thyme, chopped

Directions + Total Time: 40 min

1. Heat a pan over medium heat and warm the olive oil.

2. Sauté the onion for 3 minutes, pour in the stock, carrot, turnip, parsnip, chicken, and bay leaf.

3. Bring to a boil and simmer for 20 minutes.

4. Add in the green beans and cook for 7 minutes.

5. Discard the bay leaf, stir in the whipping cream, adjust the taste and scatter with thyme to serve.

Cal 483;

Fat 32g;

Carbs 6.9g;

Protein 33g

Indian Chicken with Mushrooms

Servings 4

Ingredients

- 1 lb chicken breasts, sliced lengthwise

- 2 tbsp butter

- 1 tbsp olive oil

- 1 cup mushrooms

- 2 cups heavy whipping cream

- 1 tbsp cilantro, chopped

- Salt and black pepper to taste

- Garam masala

- 1 tsp ground cumin

- 2 tsp ground coriander

- 1 tsp ground cardamom

- 1 tsp turmeric

- 1 tsp ginger

- 1 tsp paprika

- 1 tsp cayenne, ground

- 1 pinch ground nutmeg

Directions + Total Time: 35 min

1. Preheat oven to 370 F.

2. In a bowl, mix all the garam masala spices.

3. Coat the chicken with the mixture.

4. Heat the olive oil and butter in a frying pan over medium heat, and

5. brown the chicken for 3-5 minutes per side.

6. Transfer to a baking dish.

7. In a bowl, mix the heavy cream and mushrooms. Season with

8. salt and pepper and pour over the chicken. Bake for 20 minutes until the mixture starts to bubble. Garnish with chopped cilantro to serve.

Cal 553;

Fat 49g;

Carbs 4.5g;

Protein 32g

Chili Chicken Kebab with Garlic Dressing

Servings 4

Ingredients

- Skewers

- 2 tbsp olive oil

- 3 tbsp soy sauce, sugar-free

- 1 tbsp ginger paste

- 2 tbsp Swerve brown sugar

- Chili pepper to taste

- 2 chicken breasts, cubed

Dressing

- ½ cup tahini

- 1 tbsp parsley, chopped

- 1 garlic clove, minced

- Salt and black pepper to taste

- ¼ cup warm water

Directions + Total Time: 25 min + cooling time

1. To make the marinade, in a small bowl, whisk the soy sauce, ginger paste,

2. Swerve brown sugar, chili pepper, and olive oil.

3. Put the chicken in a zipper bag, pour the marinade over, seal and shake for an even coat.

4. Marinate in the fridge for 2 hours.

5. Preheat a grill to high heat.

6. Thread the chicken on skewers and cook for 10 minutes in total with three to four turnings to be golden brown.

7. Transfer to a plate.

8. Mix the dressing ingredients in a bowl.

9. Serve the chicken skewers topped with the tahini dressing.

Cal 410;

Fat 32g;

Carbs 4.8g;

Protein 23g

Feta & Bacon Chicken

Servings 4

Ingredients

- 4 oz bacon, chopped

- 1 lb chicken breasts

- 3 green onions, chopped

- 2 tbsp coconut oil

- 4 oz feta cheese, crumbled

- 1 tbsp parsley

Directions + Total Time: 24 min

1. Place a pan over medium heat the coconut oil.

2. Add in the bacon and cook until crispy.

3. Remove to paper towels, drain the grease, and crumble.

4. To the same pan, add the chicken breasts and cook for 4-5 minutes.

5. Flip to the other side and cook for an additional 4-5 minutes. Transfer to a baking dish.

6. Top with the green onions, set in the oven, turn on the broiler, and cook for 5 minutes at high temperature.

7. Serve topped with bacon, feta cheese, and parsley.

8. Enjoy!

Cal 459;

Fat 35g;

Net Carbs 3.1g;

Protein 32g

Pork Steaks with Carrot & Broccoli

Servings 2

Ingredients

- 1 tbsp olive oil

- 1 tbsp butter

- 2 pork steaks, bone-in

- ½ cup water

- Salt and black pepper to taste

- 2 garlic cloves, minced

- 1 tbsp fresh parsley, chopped

- ½ head broccoli, cut into florets

- 1 carrot, sliced

- ½ lemon, sliced

Directions + Total Time: 30 min

1. Heat oil and butter over high heat.

2. Add in the pork steaks, season with pepper and salt, and cook until browned; set to a plate.

3. In the same pan, add garlic, carrot, and broccoli and cook for 4 minutes.

4. Pour the water, lemon slices, salt, and black pepper and cook

5. everything for 5 minutes.

6. Return the pork steaks to the pan and cook for 10 minutes.

7. Serve the steaks sprinkled with parsley.

Cal 674;

Fat 67g;

Carbs 7.5g;

Protein 51g

Greek-Style Pork Chops

Servings 2

Ingredients

- 1 garlic clove, minced

- 2 pork chops, bone-in

- Salt and black pepper to taste

- 1 tsp dried oregano

- ¼ cup Kalamata olives, sliced

- 2 tbsp olive oil

- 2 tbsp vegetable broth

- ¼ cup feta cheese, crumbled

Directions + Total Time: 45 min

1. Preheat the oven to 425 F.

2. Rub pork chops with pepper and salt and place in a roasting pan.

3. Stir in the garlic, olives, olive oil, broth, and oregano.

4. Set in the oven and bake for 10 minutes.

5. Reduce heat to 350 F and roast for 25 minutes.

6. Plate the pork and sprinkle with pan juices and feta cheese all over.

7. Serve

8. Enjoy!

Cal 533;

Fat 38g;

Carbs 1.9g;

Protein 41g

Hot Pork Meatballs

Servings 2

Ingredients

- ¼ cup mozzarella cheese, grated

- 1 lb ground pork

- Salt and black pepper to taste

- 2 tbsp yellow mustard

- ½ cup almond flour

- ¼ cup hot sauce

- 1 egg

Directions + Total Time: 36 min

1. Preheat oven to 400 F.

2. Line a baking tray with parchment paper.

3. In a bowl, combine the pork, pepper, mustard, flour, mozzarella cheese, salt, and egg.

4. Form meatballs and arrange them on the baking tray.

5. Cook for 16-20 minutes, then pour over the hot sauce and bake for 5 more minutes.

6. Serve warm and enjoy!

Cal 487; Fat 35g; Net Carbs 4.3g; Protein 32g308.Pork Chops with

Peanut Sauce

Servings 2

Ingredients

- 1 tbsp cilantro, chopped

- 1 tbsp mint, chopped

- 1 onion, chopped

- ¼ cup peanuts

- 3 tbsp olive oil

- Salt to taste

- 2 pork chops

- 2 garlic cloves, minced

- Juice and zest from 1 lemon

Directions + Total Time: 40 min + cooling time

1. In a food processor, combine the cilantro with olive oil, mint, peanuts, salt, lemon zest, garlic, and onion.

2. Rub the pork with the mixture, place in a bowl, and refrigerate for 1 hour while covered.

3. Preheat oven to 350 F.

4. Remove the chops and set to a greased baking dish, sprinkle with lemon juice, and bake for 30 minutes in the oven.

5. Serve.

Cal 643;

Fat 47g;

Carbs 6g;

Protein 45.4g

Fried Pork with Blackberry Gravy

Servings 2

Ingredients

- 2 tbsp olive oil

- 1 lb pork chops

- Salt and black pepper to taste

- 1 cup blackberries

- 2 tbsp chicken broth

- ½ tbsp rosemary, chopped

- 1 tbsp balsamic vinegar

- 1 tsp Worcestershire sauce

Directions + Total Time: 20 min

1. Place the blackberries in a bowl and mash them with a fork until jam like.

2. Pour into a saucepan over medium heat and add the broth and rosemary.

3. Bring to boil on low heat for 4 minutes.

4. Stir in balsamic vinegar and Worcestershire sauce.

5. Simmer for 1 minute.

6. Heat the olive oil in a skillet over medium heat.

7. Season the pork with salt and pepper and cook for 5 minutes on each side.

8. Put on serving plates and spoon sauce over.

9. Enjoy!

Cal 732;

Fat 42g;

Carbs 6.9g;

Protein 56g

Beef and Lamb

Beef Ragout with Pepper & Green Beans

Servings 4

Ingredients

- 1 lb chuck steak, trimmed and cubed

- 2 tbsp olive oil

- Salt and black pepper to taste

- 2 tbsp almond flour

- 4 green onions, diced

- ½ cup dry white wine

- 1 yellow bell pepper, diced

- 1 cup green beans, chopped

- 2 tsp Worcestershire sauce

- 4 oz tomato puree

- 3 tsp smoked paprika

- 1 cup beef broth

- Parsley leaves to garnish

Directions and Total Time: approx. 2 hours

1. Dredge the meat in the almond flour and set aside.

2. Place a large skillet over medium heat, add 1 tablespoon of oil to heat and then sauté the green onion, green beans, and bell pepper for 3 minutes.

3. Stir in the paprika and the remaining olive oil.

4. Add the beef and cook for 10 minutes while turning them halfway.

5. Stir in white wine, let it reduce by half, about 3 minutes, and add

6. Worcestershire sauce, tomato puree, and beef broth.

7. Let the mixture boil for 2 minutes, then reduce the heat to lowest and let simmer for 1 ½ hours; stirring now and then.

8. Adjust the taste and dish the ragout.

9. Serve garnished with parsley.

Cal 334;

Fat 22g;

Carbs 3.9g;

Protein 33g

Grilled Beef on Skewers with Fresh Salad

Servings 2

Ingredients

- 1 lb sirloin steak, boneless, cubed
- ¼ cup ranch dressing
- 1 red onion, sliced
- ½ tbsp white wine vinegar
- 1 tbsp extra virgin olive oil
- 2 ripe tomatoes, sliced
- 2 tbsp fresh parsley, chopped
- 1 cucumber, sliced
- Salt to taste

Directions and Total Time: approx. 20 minutes

1. Thread the beef cubes on the skewers, about 4 to 5 cubes per skewer.

2. Brush half of the ranch dressing on the skewers (all around).

3. Preheat grill to high. Place the skewers on the grill and cook for 6 minutes.

4. Turn the skewers and cook further for 6 minutes. Brush the remaining ranch dressing on the meat and cook them for 1 more minute on each side.

5. In a salad bowl, mix together red onion, tomatoes, and cucumber, sprinkle with salt, vinegar, and extra virgin olive oil; toss to combine.

6. Top the salad with skewers and scatter the parsley all over.

Cal 423;

Fat 24g;

Carbs 2.4g;

Protein 45g

Beef Sausage & Okra Casserole

Servings 2

Ingredients

- ½ cup marinara sauce, sugar-free
- 1 cup okra, trimmed
- 1 tbsp olive oil
- 1 celery stalk, chopped
- ¼ cup almond flour
- 1 egg
- 1 lb beef sausage, chopped
- Salt and black pepper to taste
- ½ tbsp dried parsley
- ¼ tsp red pepper flakes
- ¼ cup Parmesan cheese, grated
- 2 green onions, chopped
- ½ tsp garlic powder
- ¼ tsp dried oregano
- ½ cup ricotta cheese
- 1 cup cheddar cheese, grated

Directions + Total Time: 35 min

1. In a bowl, combine the sausage, pepper, pepper flakes, oregano,
2. egg, Parmesan cheese, green onions, almond flour, salt, parsley,

3. celery, and garlic powder.

4. Form balls, lay them on a lined baking sheet, place in the oven at 390 F, and bake for 15 minutes.

5. Remove the balls from the oven and cover with half of the marinara sauce and okra.

6. Pour ricotta cheese all over, followed by the rest of the marinara sauce.

7. Scatter the cheddar cheese and bake in the oven for 10 minutes. Allow to cool before serving.

Cal 479;

Fat 31g;

Net Carbs 4.3g;

Protein 39g

Grilled Beef Steaks & Vegetable Medley

Servings 2

Ingredients

- 1 red bell pepper, seeded, cut into strips

- 2 sirloin beef steaks

- Salt and black pepper to taste

- 2 tbsp olive oil

- 1 ½ tbsp balsamic vinegar

- ¼ lb asparagus, trimmed

- ½ cup mushrooms, sliced

- ½ cup snow peas

- 1 small onion, quartered

- 1 garlic clove, sliced

Directions and Total Time: approx. 30 minutes

1. In a bowl, put asparagus, mushrooms, snow peas, bell pepper, onion, and garlic.

2. Mix salt, pepper, olive oil, and balsamic vinegar in a small bowl, and pour half of the mixture over the vegetables; stir to combine.

3. To the remaining oil mixture, add the beef and toss to coat well.

4. Preheat a grill pan over high heat.

5. Place the steaks in the grill pan and sear for 6-8 minutes on each side.

6. Remove the beef and set aside.

7. Pour the vegetables and marinade in the pan and cook for 5 minutes, turning once.

8. Share the vegetables into plates.

9. Top with beef and drizzle the sauce from the pan all and serve.

Cal 488;

Fat 31g;

Net Carbs 4.1g;

Protein 57g

Beef & Mushroom Meatloaf

Servings 4

Ingredients

- Meatloaf
- 1 lb ground beef
- ½ onion, chopped
- 1 tbsp almond milk
- 1 tbsp almond flour
- 1 garlic clove, minced
- 1 cup sliced mushrooms
- 1 small egg
- Salt and black pepper to taste
- 1 tbsp parsley, chopped
- ⅓ cup Parmesan cheese, grated
- Glaze
- 1/3 cup balsamic vinegar
- ¼ tbsp xylitol
- ¼ tsp tomato paste
- ¼ tsp garlic powder
- ¼ tsp onion powder
- 1 tbsp ketchup, sugar-free

Directions + Total Time: 1 h 10 min

1. Grease a loaf pan with cooking spray and set aside.

2. Preheat oven to 390 F. Combine all meatloaf ingredients in a large bowl.

3. Press this mixture into the prepared loaf pan.

4. Bake in the oven for about 30 minutes.

5. To make the glaze, whisk all ingredients in a bowl.

6. Pour the glaze over the meatloaf.

7. Put the meatloaf back in the oven and cook for 20 more minutes.

8. Let meatloaf sit for 10 minutes before slicing.

9. Serve and enjoy!

Cal 311;

Fat 21g;

Carbs 5.5g;

Protein 24g

Stewed Veal with Vegetables

Servings 4

Ingredients

- 2 tbsp olive oil
- 1 lb veal shoulder, cubed
- 1 onion, chopped
- 1 garlic clove, minced
- Salt and black pepper to taste
- ½ cup white wine
- 1 tsp sweet paprika
- 2 cups tomatoes, chopped
- 1 carrot, chopped
- 1 turnip, chopped
- ½ cup celery, chopped
- 1 cup mushrooms, chopped
- ½ cup green beans, chopped
- 1 tsp dried oregano

Directions + Total Time: 1 hour 25 min

1. Set a pot over medium heat and warm the oil.
2. Brown the veal for 5-6 minutes.
3. Stir in the onion, celery and garlic, and cook for 3 minutes.
4. Place in the wine to deglaze the bottom for 1-2 minutes.

5. Add in oregano, paprika, carrot, tomatoes, 1 cup of water, turnip,

6. mushrooms, salt, and pepper, and bring to a boil.

7. Reduce the heat to low and cook for 1 hour.

8. Add in green beans and cook for 5 minutes.

9. Serve and enjoy!

Cal 495;

Fat 22g;

Carbs 6.8g;

Protein 51g

Red Wine Lamb with Mint & Sage

Servings 4

Ingredients

- 1 tbsp olive oil

- 1 lb lamb chops

- ½ tbsp sage

- ½ tsp mint

- ½ onion, sliced

- 1 garlic clove, minced

- ¼ cup red wine

- Salt and black pepper to taste

Directions + Total Time: 45 min

1. Heat the olive oil in a pan.

2. Add onion and garlic and cook for 3 minutes, until soft.

3. Rub the sage and mint over the lamb chops.

4. Cook the lamb for about 3 minutes per side; set aside.

5. Pour the red wine and 1 cup of water into the pan, bring the mixture to a boil.

6. Cook until the liquid is reduced by half. Add the chops to the pan, reduce the heat, and let simmer for 30 minutes.

7. Adjust the seasoning and serve.

Cal 402; Fat 29g; Carbs 3.8g; Protein 15g

Lamb Chops with Garlic-Lime Vinaigrette

Servings 2

Ingredients

- 4 lamb chops
- 4 tsp olive oil
- Salt and black pepper to taste
- ½ tsp red pepper flakes
- 1 tbsp lime juice
- 1 tbsp fresh mint
- 1 garlic clove, pressed
- 1 tbsp parsley
- ½ tsp smoked paprika

Directions + Total Time: 25 min

1. Heat a griddle pan over high heat.
2. Brush the lamb with 2 tbsp of olive oil and sprinkle with salt and black pepper.
3. Grill the lamb chops for about 3-5 minutes per side.
4. Whisk together the remaining olive oil, red pepper flakes, lime juice, mint, garlic, parsley, and smoked paprika in a jar; shake until smooth and creamy.
5. Serve the lamb chops topped with the vinaigrette.

Cal 365; Fat 29g; Carbs 2.1g; Protein 25g

Stuffed Lamb Shoulder

Servings 4

Ingredients

- 1 lb rolled lamb shoulder, boneless
- 5 tbsp macadamia nuts, chopped
- 1 ½ cups basil leaves, chopped
- ½ cup green olives, chopped
- 2 garlic cloves, minced
- Salt and black pepper to taste

Directions + Total Time: 60 min

1. In a bowl, combine basil, macadamia, olives, and garlic.
2. Season lamb with salt and pepper.
3. Spread with the previously prepared mixture, roll up the lamb and tie it together using 3 strings of butcher's twine.
4. Place lamb onto a greased baking dish and cook in the oven for 45 minutes at 380 F.
5. When ready, transfer the meat to a chopping board, and let it rest for 10 minutes before slicing.
6. Serveand enjoy!

Cal 557; Fat 41g; Net Carbs 3.1g; Protein 37g

Fish and Vegetables Recipes

Greek Sea Bass with Olive Sauce

Servings 2

Ingredients

- 2 sea bass fillets

- 2 tbsp olive oil

- A pinch of chili pepper

- 1 tbsp green olives, sliced

- 1 lemon, juiced

- Salt to taste

Directions and Total Time: approx. 20 minutes

1. Preheat grill to high.

2. In a small bowl, mix together half of the olive oil, chili pepper, and salt and rub onto the sea bass fillets.

3. Grill the fish on both sides for 5-6 minutes until brown.

4. In a skillet over medium heat, warm the remaining olive oil and stir in the lemon juice, olives, and salt; cook for 3-4 minutes.

5. Plate the fillets and pour the lemon sauce over to serve.

Cal 267;

Fat 16g;

Carbs 1.6g;

Protein 24g

Parmesan Shrimp Scampi Pizza

Servings 4

Ingredients

- 3 tbsp olive oil
- 2 tbsp butter
- ½ lb shrimp, deveined
- ½ cup almond flour
- ¼ tsp salt
- 2 tbsp ground psyllium husk
- 2 garlic cloves, minced
- ¼ cup white wine
- ½ tsp dried basil
- ½ tsp dried parsley
- ½ lemon, juiced
- 2 cups grated cheese blend
- ½ tsp Italian seasoning
- ¼ cup grated Parmesan

Directions + Total Time: 30 min

1. Preheat oven to 380 F.
2. Line a baking sheet with parchment paper.
3. In a bowl, mix almond flour, salt, psyllium powder, 1 tbsp of olive oil, and 1 cup of lukewarm water until dough forms.
4. Spread the mixture on the baking sheet and bake for 10 minutes.

5. Meanwhile, heat butter and the remaining olive oil in a skillet.

6. Sauté garlic for 30 seconds.

7. Mix in the wine and cook until it reduces by half.

8. Stir in basil, parsley, and lemon juice.

9. Stir in the shrimp and cook for 3 minutes. Mix in the cheese blend and Italian seasoning.

10. Let the cheese melt, 3 minutes.

11. Spread the shrimp mixture on the crust and top with Parmesan cheese.

12. Bake for 5 minutes or until the cheese melts.

13. Slice and serve warm.

Cal 419;

Carbs 3g;

Fats 29g;

Protein 23g

Spiralized Zucchini with Garlic Shrimp

Servings 4

Ingredients

- 2 tbsp butter
- 1 lb jumbo shrimp, deveined
- 4 garlic cloves, minced
- 1 cup grated Parmesan cheese
- 1 pinch red chili flakes
- ¼ cup white wine
- 1 lime, zested and juiced
- 3 zucchinis, spiralized
- 2 tbsp chopped parsley
- Salt and black pepper to taste

Directions + Total Time:. 15 min

1. Warm the butter in a skillet and cook the shrimp for 3-4 minutes. Flip and stir in garlic and red chili flakes.
2. Cook further for 1 minute; set aside.
3. Pour the wine and lime juice into the skillet and stir to deglaze the bottom; cook until reduced by a third.
4. Mix in zucchini, lime zest, shrimp, and parsley.
5. Season with salt and pepper and cook for 2 minutes.
6. Top with Parmesan and serve.

Cal 261; Net Carbs 8.9g; Fats 8g; Protein 29g

Anchovy Caprese Pizza

Servings 4

Ingredients

- Crust

- 4 eggs

- ¼ cup buttermilk

- 2 tbsp flaxseed meal

- 1 tsp chipotle pepper

- ¼ tsp fennel seeds, ground

- ¼ tsp salt

- 1 tbsp olive oil

Topping

- 1 ball (8-oz) fresh mozzarella, sliced

- 2 tbsp tomato paste

- 4 basil leaves

- 2 tomatoes, sliced

- 2 anchovies, chopped

Directions + Total Time: 40 min

1. In a bowl, whisk the eggs, and add in buttermilk, flax seed, fennel

2. seeds, chipotle pepper, and salt.

3. Set a pan over medium heat and warm ½ tbsp of olive oil. Ladle ½ of the crust mixture into the pan and spread out evenly.

4. Cook until the edges are set; then, flip the crust and cook on the other side, 3-4 minutes.

5. Warm the remaining ½ tbsp of oil in the pan.

6. Repeat the same process with the other pizza crust.

7. Spread the crusts with tomato paste and top with fresh mozzarella and tomato slices.

8. In batches, bake in the oven for 8-10 minutes at

9. 430 F until the cheese melts. Garnish with anchovies and basil leaves.

10. Serve.

Cal 465; Fat 31g; Net Carbs 5.1g; Protein 32g

Roasted Cauliflower with Chilli Dressing

Servings 4

Ingredients

- 1 head cauliflower, chopped

- 3 tbsp olive oil

- 1 tbsp chili oil

- 1 lemon, zested and juiced

- 1 tbsp red chili flake

- 2 tbsp capers, drained

- 2 tbsp cilantro, chopped

- Salt and black pepper to taste

Directions and Total Time: approx. 35 minutes

1. Preheat oven to 360 F. Place the cauliflower in a baking dish and

2. drizzle half of the olive oil all over.

3. Season with salt and pepper.

4. Roast until golden, 20-25 minutes.

5. In a bowl, whisk the remaining olive oil, chili oil, lemon zest, lemon juice, and salt.

6. Stir in capers and red chili flakes.

7. Remove the cauliflower to a serving plate and drizzle with the dressing.

8. Sprinkle with cilantro and serve warm.

Cal 138; Carbs 1.6g; Fat 14g; Protein 1.4g

Cheddar Stuffed Zucchini

Servings 2

Ingredients

- 4 tbsp butter

- 1 zucchini, halved

- 1 ½ oz baby kale

- 2 garlic cloves, minced

- 2 tbsp tomato sauce

- 1 cup cheddar cheese

- Salt and black pepper to taste

Directions +Total Time: 40 min

1. Preheat oven to 375 F.

2. Scoop out zucchini pulp with a spoon.

3. Keep the flesh. Grease a baking sheet with cooking spray and place in the zucchini boats.

4. Melt butter in a skillet over medium heat and sauté garlic until fragrant and slightly browned, 4 minutes.

5. Add in kale and zucchini pulp. Cook until the kale wilts; season with salt and pepper.

6. Spoon tomato sauce into the boats and spread to coat evenly.

7. Top with kale mixture and sprinkle with cheddar cheese.

8. Bake for 25 minutes.

Cal 617; Carbs 4g; Fat 61g; Protein 19g

Butternut Squash Roast with Chimichurri

Servings 4

Ingredients

- 1 lb butternut squash

- 1 tbsp butter, melted

- 3 tbsp toasted pine nuts

- Salt and black pepper to taste

- Chimichurri:

- Zest and juice of 1 lemon

- 1 jalapeño pepper, chopped

- 1 cup olive oil

- 2 garlic cloves, minced

- ½ cup chopped fresh parsley

- ½ red bell pepper, chopped

Directions and Total Time: approx. 25 minutes

1. Add all the chimichurri ingredients to a food processor and grind until desired consistency is achieved; adjust the seasoning.

2. Keep in the fridge until ready to use.

3. Slice the squash into rounds and remove the seeds.

4. Drizzle with butter and season with salt and pepper. Preheat a grill pan over medium heat and cook the squash for 5-6 minutes on each side.

5. Scatter pine nuts on top and serve with chimichurri.

Cal 647;

Carbs 6g;

Fat 44g;

Protein 49g

Roasted Pepper with Tofu

Servings 4

Ingredients

- 2 ½ cups cubed tofu

- 4 orange bell peppers

- 1 cucumber, diced

- 1 large tomato, chopped

- 3 oz cream cheese

- ¾ cup mayonnaise

- 1 tbsp melted butter

- 1 tsp dried parsley

- 1 tsp dried basil

- Salt and black pepper to taste

Directions and Total Time: approx. 25 minutes

1. Preheat a broiler to 450 F.

2. Line a baking sheet with parchment paper.

3. In a salad bowl, combine cream cheese, mayonnaise, cucumber, tomato, salt, pepper, and parsley; refrigerate.

4. Arrange bell peppers and tofu on the baking sheet, drizzle with melted butter, and season with basil, salt, and pepper.

5. Bake for 15 minutes until the peppers have charred lightly and the tofu browned.

6. Serve with chilled salad and enjoy!

Cal 838;

Net Carbs 8g;

Fat 81g;

Protein 31g

Dessert and Snacks

Coconut Panna Cotta with Raspberries

Servings 5

Ingredients

- 12 fresh raspberries
- 2 cups coconut cream
- ½ tbsp powdered gelatin
- ¼ tsp vanilla extract
- 1 tsp turmeric
- 1 tbsp erythritol
- 1 tbsp chopped toasted pecans

Directions + Total Time: 15 min + chilling time

1. Combine gelatin and ½ tsp water in a bowl and allow sitting to dissolve.
2. Pour coconut cream, vanilla extract, turmeric, and erythritol into a saucepan and bring to a boil; simmer for 2 minutes.
3. Turn the heat off. Stir in gelatin mixture.
4. Pour into 6 glasses, cover with a plastic wrap, and refrigerate for 2 hours.
5. Top with pecans and raspberries and serve.

Cal 269;

Carbs 3g;

Fat 31g;

Ricotta Parfait with Strawberries

Servings 4

Ingredients

- 1 cup ricotta cheese

- 2 cups strawberries, chopped

- 2 tbsp sugar-free maple syrup

- 2 tbsp balsamic vinegar

Directions + Total Time: 10 min

1. Distribute half of the strawberries between 4 small glasses and top

2. with ricotta cheese.

3. Drizzle with maple syrup and balsamic vinegar and finish with the remaining strawberries.

4. Serve.

Cal 159;

Carbs 3.1g;

Fats 8g;

Protein 6.9g

Minty Coconut Parfait with Cranberries

Servings 4

Ingredients

- 1 cup fresh cranberries

- 2 tbsp hemp seeds

- 2 cups coconut yogurt

- ½ lemon, zested

- 3 mint sprigs, chopped

- Sugar-free maple syrup to taste

Directions + Total Time: 10 min

1. Spoon half of coconut yogurt into 4 serving glasses. Top with cranberries, lemon zest, and hemp seeds.

2. Cover with the remaining coconut yogurt and drizzle with maple syrup.

3. Sprinkle with chopped mint and serve.

Cal 98;

Carbs 2.9g,

Fat 7.8g,

Protein 4.7g

Healthy Chia Pudding With Strawberries

Servings 4

Ingredients

- 1 cup yogurt, full-fat
- 2 tsp xylitol
- 2 tbsp chia seeds
- 1 cup fresh strawberries, sliced
- 1 tbsp lemon zest
- 2 mint leaves, chopped

Directions + Total Time: 15 min + chilling time

1. In a bowl, combine the yogurt and xylitol together.
2. Add in the chia seeds and stir.
3. Reserve a couple of strawberries for garnish, and mash the remaining ones with a fork until pureed.
4. Stir in the yogurt mixture and refrigerate for 45 minutes.
5. Once cooled, divide the mixture between dessert glasses.
6. Top each with the reserved slices of strawberries, mint leaves, and lemon zest.
7. Serve.

Cal 187;

Fat 11g;

Carbs 6.3g;

Protein 6.7g

Chocolate Candies with Blueberries

Servings 4

Ingredients

- 1 ½ cups blueberry preserves, sugar-free

- 10 oz unsweetened chocolate chips

- 2 cups raw cashew nuts

- 2 tbsp ground flax seeds

- 3 tbsp xylitol

- 3 tbsp olive oil

Directions + Total Time: 10 min + cooling time

1. Grind the cashew nuts and flax seeds in a blender for 50 seconds

2. until smoothly crushed; add the blueberries and 2 tbsp of xylitol.

3. Process further for 1 minute until well combined. Form 1-inch balls of the mixture.

4. Line a baking sheet with parchment paper and place the balls on the baking sheet.

5. Freeze for 1 hour or until firmed up. In your microwave, melt the chocolate chips, olive oil, and the remaining xylitol for 95 seconds.

6. Toss the truffles to coat in the chocolate mixture, put on the baking sheet, and freeze up for at least 3 hours.

Cal 253; Fat 18g; Carbs 4.1g; Protein 10g

www.ingramcontent.com/pod-product-compliance
Lightning Source LLC
Chambersburg PA
CBHW050626070726
47592CB00028B/1073